Date: 4/27/12

NATURE'S
LIFE
Cycles

The Life Cycle
of a
HONEYBEE

By Barbara M. Linde

Gareth Stevens
Publishing

Please visit our Web site, www.garethstevens.com. For a free color catalog of all our high-quality books, call toll free 1-800-542-2595 or fax 1-877-542-2596.

Library of Congress Cataloging-in-Publication Data

Linde, Barbara M.
 The life cycle of a honeybee / Barbara M. Linde.
     p. cm. — (Nature's life cycles)
 Includes index.
 ISBN 978-1-4339-4676-9 (pbk.)
 ISBN 978-1-4339-4677-6 (6-pack)
 ISBN 978-1-4339-4675-2 (library binding)
 1. Honeybee—Life cycles—Juvenile literature. I. Title.
 SF523.5.L56 2011
 638'.12–dc22

                                        2010029688

First Edition

Published in 2011 by
Gareth Stevens Publishing
111 East 14th Street, Suite 349
New York, NY 10003

Copyright © 2011 Gareth Stevens Publishing

Designer: Daniel Hosek
Editor: Therese Shea

Photo credits: Cover, pp. 1, 5, 7, 19, 20, 21 (adult) Shutterstock.com; pp. 9, 11, 15, 21 (larva) iStockphoto.com; pp. 11 (egg inset), 13, 17, 21 (pupa, egg) Oxford Scientific/Getty Images.

Printed in the United States of America

CPSIA compliance information: Batch #CW11GS: For further information contact Gareth Stevens, New York, New York at 1-800-542-2595.

Contents

Words in the glossary appear in **bold** type the first time they are used in the text.

What Is a Honeybee?

A honeybee is an **insect**. Two **antennae** on its head help the bee smell. It has five eyes. Two large eyes see shapes and colors. Three small eyes can tell light from dark.

The middle part of a honeybee's body is called the thorax. Three pairs of legs and two pairs of wings are connected to the thorax. A honeybee's wings make the bee's buzzing sound.

A stinger is attached to each female bee's stomach, or abdomen. Males don't have stingers.

A honeybee leaves its stinger behind when it stings. Then it dies.
▼

Honeybee Homes

Honeybees live almost all over the world. They live in groups called colonies. Most honeybees live in the wild. They like to make their home in a dark, dry place above the ground. They may set up a colony in a hollow log, a cave, or a crack in a rock. Their home is called a hive.

People called beekeepers raise honeybees in special wooden boxes. Drawers make it easy to collect honey from the bees.

AWESOME ANIMAL!

Honeybees can fly 15 miles (24 km) an hour! That's about as fast as a person can ride a bike.

A colony may have as many as 70,000 bees!

Kinds of Honeybees

Each hive has three kinds of honeybees. Each kind has certain jobs. Most of the honeybees are female worker bees. There can be tens of thousands in a colony. Male honeybees are called drones. There may be 200 to 300 drones. There's usually only one queen in a hive.

Each honeybee's life cycle has four stages: egg, **larva**, **pupa**, and adult. The honeybee changes from one stage to the next. This process of changing is called **metamorphosis**.

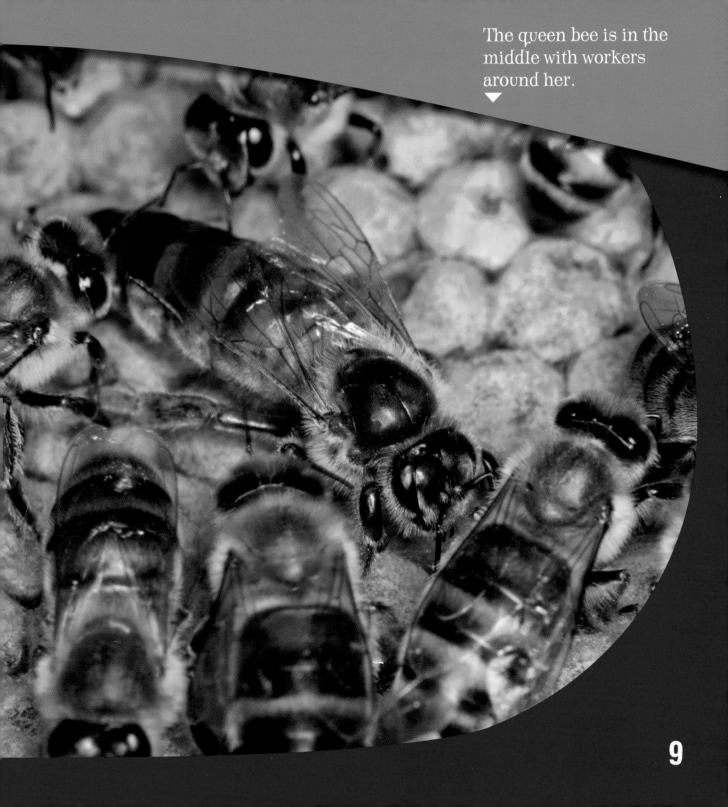

The queen bee is in the
middle with workers
around her.
▼

Egg to Larva

Inside the hive, some worker bees create a honeycomb using beeswax made in their bodies. The honeycomb is made up of small six-sided rooms called cells. Some cells hold eggs.

The queen bee **mates** with a drone. Then she lays eggs in the cells. After about 3 days, a larva comes out of each egg. It looks like a tiny worm. Worker bees feed a larva for 7 to 11 days. Then they close the cell with wax. Inside the cell, the larva spins a cocoon.

AWESOME ANIMAL!

A honeybee egg is about the size of the head of a pin!

As the larva grows
larger, it loses its skin.
▼

egg

11

Larva to Pupa

Inside the cocoon, the larva becomes a pupa. Honeybees stay in this stage for 6 to 10 days.

The pupa begins to look like an adult bee, but it's white. Body parts, including the wings, grow to full size. Finally, the pupa chews through the wax in the cell. An adult bee crawls out. The metamorphosis is complete!

Even before the bee comes out of the cell, it knows if it's a worker, drone, or queen.

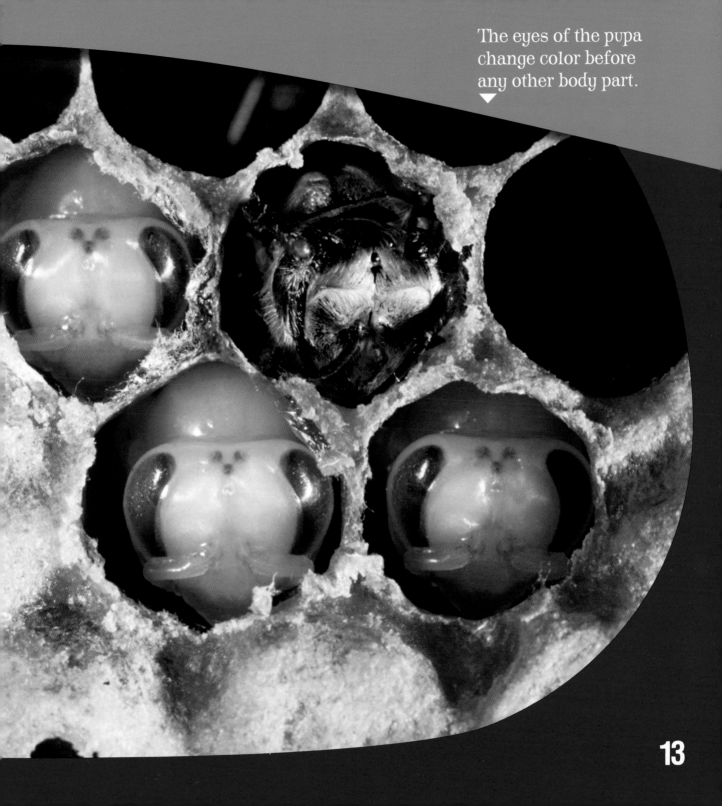

The eyes of the pupa change color before any other body part.

Queens and Drones

The queen bee gives off a special smell that tells other honeybees in the hive how to do their jobs. When the queen bee is about 1 week old, she begins to mate with drones. She usually mates with drones from other hives. The queen lives 3 to 5 years.

A drone bee's only job is to mate. Drones die after mating. Drones that don't mate are forced out of the hive and die.

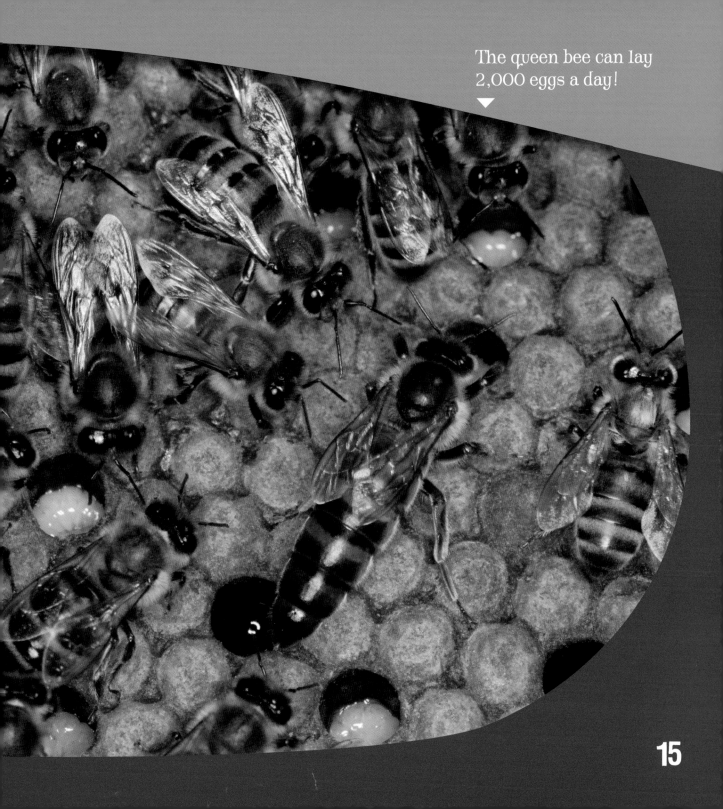

The queen bee can lay 2,000 eggs a day!

The Workers

About 2 weeks after they come out of their eggs, worker bees begin to use wax from their abdomens to build the honeycomb. They clean and guard the hive. If the hive gets too hot, they fan their wings to cool it off.

Worker bees feed the other bees. A worker bee has a tube in its mouth. The tube sucks up **nectar** from flowers. The nectar is taken to the honeycomb. Other workers change it to honey. The bees eat the honey, and so do people!

AWESOME ANIMAL!

"Royal jelly" is the name for a milky food that helps a bee larva become a queen bee.

Worker bees place food in cells for other bees to eat.

17

Flower Power

After a worker bee finds nectar, it returns to the hive. It does a "waggle dance" for the bees there. The dance tells other worker bees where to find the nectar.

When a worker bee lands on a flower, **pollen** sticks to its fuzzy body. When the bee lands on another flower, the pollen from the first flower mixes with the pollen from the second flower. This is called pollination. It helps make new flowers.

AWESOME ANIMAL!

A worker bee will make just one drop of honey during its life!

Honeybees use pollen
to make food.
▼

19

Honeybees in Danger

For over 50 million years, honeybees have been on Earth. In 2006, many honeybee colonies began to disappear. Some people think the bees got sick. Tiny insects called mites can attach to honeybees and kill them. People use sprays that keep bugs away from their gardens. These sprays may have harmed honeybees, too.

Now some communities have gardens and fields for honeybees. The number of bees seems to be growing again.

New bug sprays can be used to help plants without harming honeybees.

The Life Cycle of a Honeybee

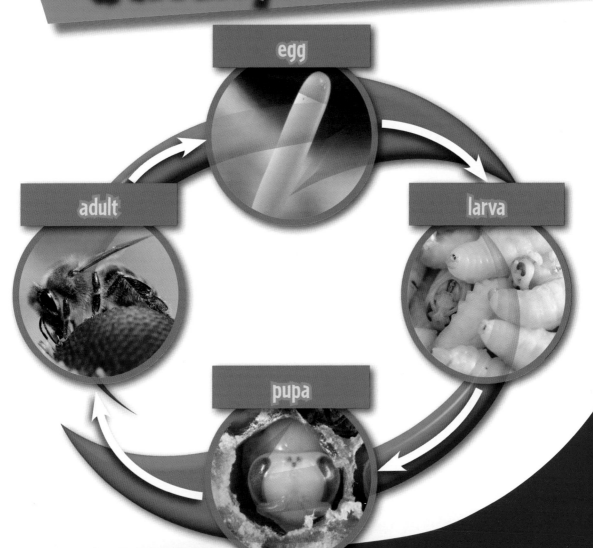

egg

larva

adult

pupa

Glossary

antenna: one of two thin, movable body parts found on the heads of some animals. The plural is "antennae."

insect: an animal that has three body parts, two antennae, two pairs of wings, three pairs of legs, and no backbone

larva: a wingless, worm-shaped form of many insects before the pupa stage

mate: coming together to make babies

metamorphosis: the changes some animals go through as they become adults

nectar: sweet liquid inside a flowering plant

pollen: a powder made by flowering plants

pupa: an insect at the stage between larva and adult, during which it builds a cocoon around itself

For More Information

Books

Mortensen, Lori. *In the Trees, Honeybees*. Nevada City, CA: Dawn Publications, 2009.

Rockwell, Anne F. *Honey in a Hive*. New York, NY: HarperCollins, 2005.

Stewart, Melissa. *How Do Bees Make Honey?* New York, NY: Marshall Cavendish Benchmark, 2009.

Web Sites

Backyard Beekeepers Association: Facts About Honeybees
www.backyardbeekeepers.com/facts.html
Check out some interesting facts about honeybees and honeybee products.

The British Beekeepers' Association
www.britishbee.org.uk/articles/life_cycle_apis_mellifera.php
Read more about the life cycles of worker, drone, and queen bees.

Index